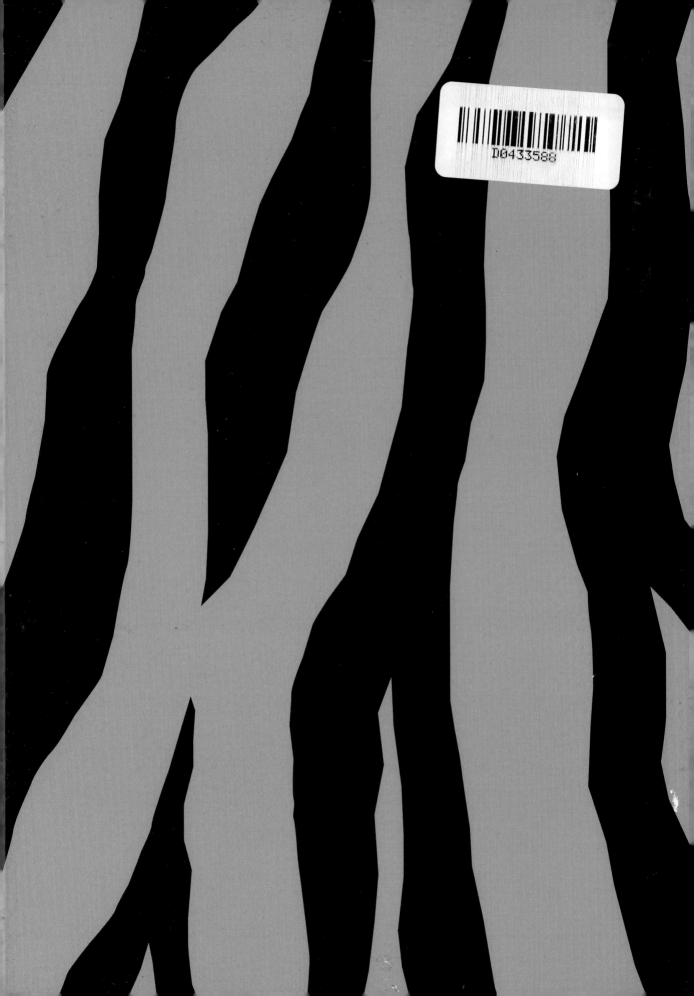

THIS BOOK BELONGS TO

....

....

....

The Puffin Book of Amazing Animal Poems

VIKING/PUFFIN

Published by the Penguin Group
Penguin Books Ltd, 27 Wrights Lane, London W8 5TZ, England
Penguin Putnam Inc., 375 Hudson Street, New York, New York 10014, USA
Penguin Books Australia Ltd, Ringwood, Victoria, Australia
Penguin Books Canada Ltd, 10 Alcorn Avenue, Toronto, Ontario, Canada M4V 3B2
Penguin Books (NZ) Ltd, Private Bag 102902, NSMC, Auckland, New Zealand

On the World Wide Web at: www.penguin.com

Penguin Books Ltd, Registered Offices: Harmondsworth, Middlesex, England

First published 2000
1 3 5 7 9 10 8 6 4 2

Set in Futura Book

Made and printed in Italy by de Agostini

British Library Cataloguing in Publication Data
A CIP catalogue record for this book is available from the British Library

ISBN 0–670–89126–6

The Puffin Book of Amazing Animal Poems

Puffin Books

CONTENTS

ENORMOUS, SHAGGY, FRIENDLY AND WAGGY
Illustrated by John Wallace

GIRAFFES, SCARVES AND LAUGHS
Illustrated by Andi Moulton

MUFFINS FOR PUFFINS
Illustrated by Ann Kronheimer

A GIGGLING GAGGLE OF GEESE
Illustrated by Nicola Smee

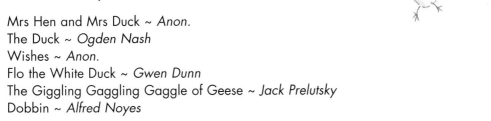

MICE ARE RATHER NICE
Illustrated by Sarah Nayler

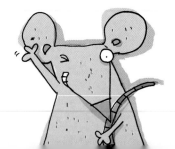

IF ONLY PIGS COULD FLY
Illustrated by Ian Cunliffe

OUR HAMSTER'S LIFE

Our hamster's life:
there's not much
to it,
not much
to it.

He presses his pink nose
to the door of his cage
and decides for the fifty six
millionth time
that he can't get
through it.

Our hamster's life:
there's not much
to it,
not much
to it.

It's about the most boring
life in the world
if he only
knew it.
He sleeps and he drinks and he eats.
He eats and he drinks and he sleeps.

He slinks and he dreeps.
He eats.

This process
he repeats.

Our hamster's life:
there's not much
to it,
not much
to it.

You'd think it would drive him bonkers,
going round and round on his wheel.
It's certainly driving me bonkers,

watching him
do it.

But he may be thinking:
'That boy's life,
there's not much
to it,
not much
to it:

watching a hamster go round on a wheel,
it's driving me bonkers if he only knew it,

watching him
watching me
do it.'

Kit Wright

ALLEY CAT

A bit of jungle in the street
He goes on velvet toes,
And slinking through the shadows, stalks
Imaginary foes.

Esther Valck Georges

I HAD A LITTLE CAT

I had a little cat called Tim Tom Tay,
I took him to town on market day,
I combed his whiskers, I brushed his tail,
I wrote on a label, 'Cat for Sale.
Knows how to deal with rats and mice.
Two pounds fifty. Bargain price.'

But when the people came to buy
I saw such a look in Tim Tom's eye
That it was clear as clear could be
I couldn't sell Tim for a fortune's fee.
I was shamed and sorry, I'll tell you plain,
And I took home Tim Tom Tay again.

Charles Causley

SUNNING

Old Dog lay in the summer sun
Much too lazy to rise and run.
He flapped an ear
At a buzzing fly;
He winked a half-opened
Sleepy eye;
He scratched himself
On an itching spot;
As he dozed on the porch
When the sun was hot.
He whimpered a bit
From force of habit,
While he lazily dreamed
Of chasing a rabbit.
But Old Dog happily lay in the sun,
Much too lazy to rise and run.

James S. Tippett

MY MUM WON'T LET ME KEEP A RABBIT

Mum won't let me keep a rabbit,
She won't let me keep a bat,
She won't let me keep a porcupine
Or a water-rat.

I can't keep pigeons
And I can't keep snails,
I can't keep kangaroos
Or wallabies with nails.

She won't let me keep a rattle-snake
Or viper in the house,
She won't let me keep a mamba
Or its meal, a mouse.

She won't let me keep a wombat
And it isn't very clear
Why I can't keep iguanas,
Jelly-fish or deer.

I can't keep a cockroach
Or a bumble-bee,
I can't keep an earwig,
A maggot or a flea.

I can't keep a wildebeest
And it's just my luck
I can't keep a mallard,
A dabchick or a duck.

She won't let me keep piranhas,
Toads or even frogs,
She won't let me keep an octopus
Or muddy water-hogs.

So out in the garden I keep a pet ant
And up in the attic
!TNAHPELE TERCES A

Brian Patten

MY NEW RABBIT

We brought him home, I was so pleased,
We made a rabbit-hutch,
I give him oats, I talk to him,
I love him very much.

Now when I talk to Rover dog,
He answers me 'Bow-wow!'
And when I speak to Pussy-cat,
She purrs and says 'Mee-ow!'

But Bunny never says a word,
Just twinkles with his nose,
And what that rabbit thinks about,
Why! no one ever knows.

My Mother says the fairies must
Have put on him a spell,
They told him all their secrets, then
They whispered, 'Pray don't tell.'

So Bunny sits there looking wise,
And twinkling with his nose,
And never, never, never tells
A single thing he knows.

Elizabeth Gould

MY RABBIT

My rabbit
has funny habits.

When I say sit
he sits.

When he hears me call
he wags
his tail a bit.

When I throw a ball
he grabs it.

What a funny rabbit!

One day in the park
I swore I heard him bark.

John Agard

I Wish I Had a Pony

I wish I had a pony
with a gold and silver mane
I'd ride him in the sunshine
I'd ride him in the rain
I'd ride him to the moon and back
and gallop around the sun
I wouldn't take him home again
until the day was done.

P. H. Kilby

Hamsters

Hamsters are the nicest things
That anyone could own.
I like them even better than
Some dogs that I have known.

Their fur is soft, their faces nice.
They're small when they are grown.
And they sit inside your pocket
When you are all alone.

Marci Ridlon

GIRAFFES,
SCARVES AND
LAUGHS

Jungle and
Wild Animals

THE DENTIST AND THE CROCODILE

The crocodile with a cunning smile,
  sat in the dentist's chair.
He said, 'Right here and everywhere
  my teeth require repair.'
The dentist's face was turning white.
  He quivered, quaked and shook.
He muttered, 'I suppose I'm going
  to have to take a look.'
'I want you,' Crocodile declared,
  'to do the back ones first.
The molars at the very back
  are easily the worst.'
He opened wide his massive jaws.
  It was a fearsome sight –
At least three hundred pointed teeth,
  all sharp and shining white.
The dentist kept himself well clear.
  He stood two yards away.
He chose the longest probe he had
  to search out the decay.
'I said to do the *back ones* first!'
  the Crocodile called out.

'You're much too far away, dear sir,
  to see what you're about.
To do the back ones properly
  you've got to put your head
Deep down inside my great big mouth,'
  the grinning Crocky said.
The poor old dentist wrung his hands
  and, weeping in despair,
He cried, 'No no! I see them all
  extremely well from here!'
Just then, in burst a lady,
  in her hands a golden chain.
She cried, 'Oh Croc, you naughty boy,
  you're playing tricks again!'
'Watch out!' the dentist shrieked and
  started climbing up the wall.
'He's after me! He's after you!
  He's going to eat us all!'
'Don't be a twit,' the lady said,
  and flashed a gorgeous smile.
'He's harmless. He's my little pet,
  my lovely crocodile.'

Roald Dahl

HOW DOTH THE LITTLE CROCODILE

How doth the little crocodile
Improve his shining tail,
And pour the waters of the Nile
On every golden scale!

How cheerfully he seems to grin,
How neatly spreads his claws,
And welcomes little fishes in
With gently smiling jaws!

Lewis Carroll

IF YOU SHOULD MEET A CROCODILE

If you should meet a crocodile
Don't take a stick and poke him
Ignore the welcome in his smile
Be careful not to stroke him
For as he sleeps upon the Nile
He thinner gets and thinner
So whenever you meet a crocodile
He's ready for his dinner!

Anon.

hmmmm...

The Hippopotamus

Consider the poor hippopotamus,
His life is unduly monotonous.
He lives half asleep
At the edge of the deep,
And his face is as big as his bottom is.

Anon.

Not a Hippopotamus

The old grey hippopotamus
Can't understand the likes of us,
He baths himself in pools of mud
Because it's cooling to his blood.
But as for us we know we ought to
Have our baths in clean hot water.
So please don't cry and make a fuss
When mother puts you in the suds:
Remember that you're one of us,
And not a hippopotamus.

A. Depledge

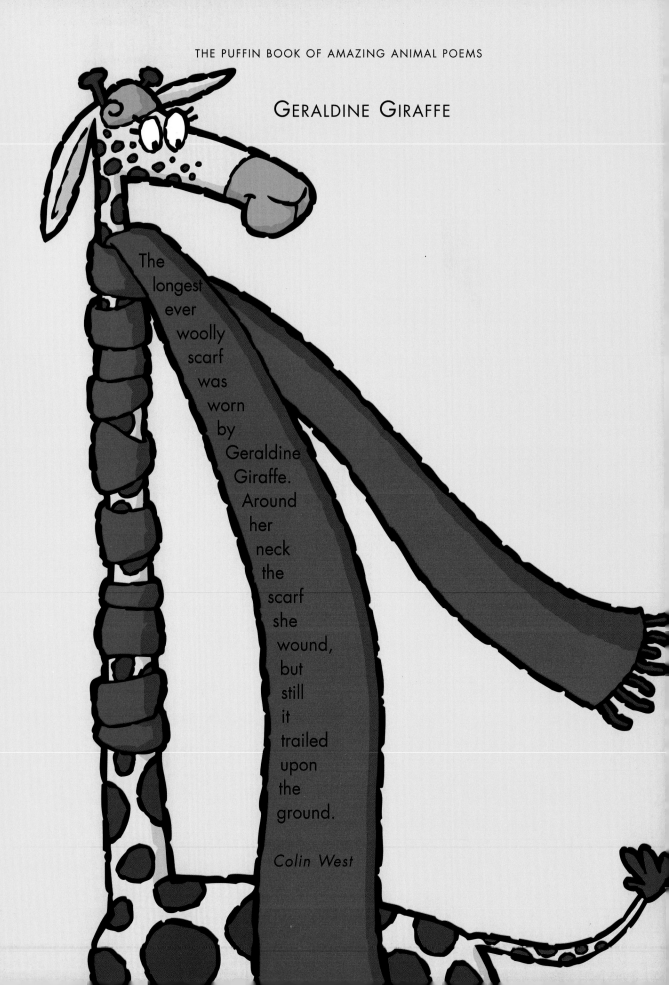

GERALDINE GIRAFFE

The
longest
ever
woolly
scarf
was
worn
by
Geraldine
Giraffe.
Around
her
neck
the
scarf
she
wound,
but
still
it
trailed
upon
the
ground.

Colin West

MR GIRAFFE

O Mister Giraffe, you make me laugh,
You seem to be made all wrong;
Your head is so high up there in the sky
And your neck is so very long
That your dinner and tea, it seems to me,
Have such a long way to go,
And I'm wondering how they manage to know
The way to your tummy below.

Geoffrey Lapage

THE LION

The lion has a golden mane
and under it a clever brain.
He lies around and idly roars
and lets the lioness do the chores.

Jack Prelutsky

IF YOU WISH TO DESCEND FROM A CAMEL

If you wish to descend from a camel,
That oddly superior mammal,
You just have to jump
From that hump on its rump;
For he won't just stop like a tram will.

Anon.

IT'S DARK IN HERE

I am writing these poems
From inside a lion,
And it's rather dark in here.
So please excuse the handwriting
Which may not be too clear.
But this afternoon by the lion's cage
I'm afraid I got too near.
And I'm writing these lines
From inside a lion,
And it's rather dark in here.

Shel Silverstein

THE YAK

Yickity-yackity, yickity-yak,
the yak has a scriffly, scraffily back;
some yaks are brown yaks and some yaks are black,
yickity-yakity, yickity-yak.

Sniggildy-snaggildy, sniggildy-snag,
the yak is all covered with shiggildy-shag;
he walks with a ziggildy-zaggildy-zag,
sniggildy-snaggildy, sniggildy-snag.

Yickity-yackity, yickity-yak,
the yak has a scriffly, scraffily back;
some yaks are brown yaks and some yaks are black,
yickity-yakity, yickity-yak.

Jack Prelutsky

THE SLOTH

In moving-slow he has no Peer.
You ask him something in his ear;
He thinks about it for a Year;

And then, before he says a Word
There, upside down (unlike a bird)
He will assume that you have Heard –

A most Ex-as-per-at-ing Lug.
But should you call his manner Smug,
He'll sigh and give his Branch a Hug;

Then off again to Sleep he goes;
Still swaying gently by his Toes,
And you just *know* he knows he knows.

Theodore Roethke

MONKEY

Have you ever watched a monkey
Climbing up a tree?
He can reach the tip-most top-most
Before you count to three.
And those who try to catch him
Just haven't got a chance.
Off he goes like a man in space
A monkey grin on his monkey face,
Legs and tail all over the place
And lands on another branch.
A cow may moo and a bee may buzz
But none can jump like a monkey does!

Herbert Kretzmer

what did
I do?

WAY DOWN SOUTH

Way down South where bananas grow
A grasshopper stepped on an elephant's toe
The elephant said, with tears in his eyes
'Pick on somebody your own size!'

Anon.

WHEN THERE'S A FIRE IN THE JUNGLE

When there's a fire in the jungle,
They call the Elephant Brigade,
Who race with their trunks full of water,
To the place that has to be sprayed.
But if the fire is a big one,
It happens as often as not,
That the elephants drink all the water,
To stop themselves getting too hot.

Martin Honeysett

THE ELEPHANT

The elephant carries a great big trunk;
He never packs it with clothes;
It has no lock and it has no key,
But he takes it wherever he goes.

Anon.

STRIPEY TIGER

A tiger has stripes
From its head to its tail,
A polar bear hasn't,
Nor has a whale.

A panda is patchy,
A leopard has spots,
A giraffe's sort of blotchy,
A deer has white dots.

An elephant's grey
And a fox is all red,
But a tiger has stripes
From his tail to his head.

Daphne Lister

HOLDING HANDS

Elephants walking
Along the trails

Are holding hands
By holding tails.

Trunks and tails
Are handy things

When elephants walk
In circus rings.

Elephants work
And elephants play

And elephants walk
And feel so gay.

And when they walk–
It never fails

They're holding hands
By holding tails.

Lenore M. Link

33

THE KANGAROO

Old Jumpety-Bumpety-Hop-and-Go-One
Was lying asleep on his side in the sun.
This old kangaroo, he was whisking the flies
(With his long glossy tail) from his ears and his eyes.
Jumpety-Bumpety-Hop-and-Go-One
Was lying asleep on his side in the sun.
Jumpety-Bumpety-Hop!

Traditional Australian

ROW, ROW

Row, row, row your boat
Gently down the stream.
If you see a crocodile,
Don't forget to SCREAM!

Traditional

MUFFINS FOR PUFFINS

Bird Poems

THE HAWK

Afternoon,
with just enough of a breeze
  for him to ride it
lazily, a hawk
sails still-winged
up the slope of a stubble-covered hill,
so low
he nearly
touches his shadow

Robert Sund

THE EAGLE

He clasps the crag with crooked hands:
Close to the sun in lonely lands,
Ringed with the azure world, he stands.

The wrinkled sea beneath him crawls;
He watches from his mountain walls,
And like a thunderbolt he falls.

Alfred, Lord Tennyson

THE REASON FOR THE PELICAN

The reason for the pelican
Is difficult to see;
His beak is clearly larger
Than there's any need to be.

It's not to bail a boat with –
He doesn't own a boat.
Yet everywhere he takes himself
He has that beak to tote.

It's not to keep his wife in –
His wife has got one, too.
It's not a scoop for eating soup.
It's not an extra shoe.

It isn't quite for anything.
And yet you realize
It's really quite a splendid beak
In quite a splendid size.

John Ciardi

I'LL BUY A PEACOCK BIRD

When I have a beard that's curly and weird,
I'll buy myself a peacock bird.
He'll shout, 'Hello, hello, hello,'
As on my lawns he'll to and fro.
Other birds will hop and glare
As he sheds feathers here and there.

I'll ask my Aunty Maud to tea
(For she has swans and a maple tree)
To view my peacock on my lawn
Who shouts 'Hello' from break of dawn,
And spy his mantle spreading wide
All shimmering blue and golden-eyed.

Modwena Sedgwick

A LITTLE BIRD'S SONG

Sometimes I've seen,
Sometimes I've heard,
Up in the tree
A little bird,
Singing a song,
A song to me,
A little brown bird
Up in the tree.
Sometimes he stays,
Sometimes he sings,
Then to the wind
He spreads his wings,
Flying away,
Away from me,
A little brown bird
Up in the tree.

Margaret Rose

CUCKOO!

Full early in the morning
Awakes the summer sun,
The month of June arriving,
The cold and night are done;
The cuckoo is a fine bird,
She whistles as she flies,
And as she whistles 'cuckoo',
The bluer grow the skies.

Anon.

THE COMMON CORMORANT

The common cormorant or shag
Lays eggs inside a paper bag.
The reason you will see no doubt
It is to keep the lightning out.
But what these unobservant birds
Have noticed is that herds
Of wandering bears may come with buns
And steal the bags to hold the crumbs.

Christopher Isherwood

THE SWALLOW

Fly away, fly away, over the sea,
Sun-loving swallow, for summer is done.
Come again, come again, come back to me,
Bringing the summer and bringing the sun.

Christina Rossetti

PENGUIN'S PROBLEM

Penguin had a problem
Penguin was upset,
The problem with Penguin was,
He hated getting wet!

Walrus tried to help him,
By teaching him to swim,
But Penguin only paddled –
He wouldn't venture in.

It's hard to be a penguin
If you're not a brilliant swimmer,
It's hard to find the fish
You have to catch to eat for dinner.

Penguin solved the problem,
Penguin learned to float –
He bought himself a fishing rod,
And built himself a boat.

Cathy Horton

CROWS

I like to walk,
And hear the black crows talk.

I like to lie
And watch crows sail the sky.

I like the crow
That wants the wind to blow:

I like the one
That thinks the wind is fun.

I like to see
Crows spilling from a tree,

And try to find
The top crow left behind.

I like to hear
Crows caw that spring is near.

I like the great
Wild clamour of crow hate

Three farms away
When owls are out by day.

I like the slow
Tired home-ward flying crow;

I like the sight
Of crows for my good-night.

David McCord

MRS PECK-PIGEON

Mrs Peck-Pigeon
Is picking for bread,
Bob-bob-bob
Goes her little round head.
Tame as a pussy-cat
In the street,
Step-step-step
Go her little red feet.
With her little red feet
And her little round head,
Mrs Peck-Pigeon
Goes picking for bread.

Eleanor Farjeon

RABBIT AND LARK

'Under the ground
It's rumbly and dark
And interesting,'
Said Rabbit to Lark.

Said Lark to Rabbit,
'Up in the sky
There's plenty of room
And it's airy and high.'

'Under the ground
It's warm and dry.
Won't you live with me?'
Was Rabbit's reply.

'The air's so sunny.
I wish you'd agree,'
Said the little Lark,
'To live with me.'

But under the ground
And up in the sky,
Larks can't burrow
Nor rabbits fly.

So Skylark over
And Rabbit under
They had to settle
To live asunder.

And often these two friends
Meet with a will
For a chat together
On top of the hill.

James Reeves

THE BIRDWATCHER'S FIRST NOTEBOOK

Monday – to the reservoir,
Real beginner's luck,
Saw a quack-quack-quacking thing,
Think it was a . . . grebe.

Tuesday – to the farmyard,
Only mud, but then
Saw a cluck-cluck-clucking thing,
Think it was a . . . partridge.

Wednesday – out at midnight,
Tom-cats on the prowl,
Heard a twit-twit-twooing thing,
Think it was a . . . nightingale.

Thursday – to the seaside,
Weather grey and dull,
Saw a big white wailing thing,
Think it was a . . . spoonbill.

Friday – brown bird on the lawn,
Outside in a rush,
Saw a worm tug-tugging thing,
Think it was . . . pipit.

Saturday – to the heathery moon
Scanned the sky and hark!
Heard a trill-trill-trilling thing,
Think it was a . . . curlew.

Sunday – tired of birdwatching,
Made a bamboo wicket,
Asked some friends round, cadged a bat,
Had a game of . . . football.

Richard Edwards

DUCK'S DITTY

All along the backwater,
Through the rushes tall,
Ducks are a-dabbling,
Up tails all!

Ducks' tails, drakes' tails,
Yellow feet a-quiver,
Yellow bills all out of sight
Busy in the river!

Slushy green undergrowth
Where the roach swim,
Here we keep our larder
Cool and full and dim!

Every one for what he likes!
We like to be
Heads down, tails up,
Dabbling free!

High in the blue above
Swifts whirl and call –
We are down a-dabbling,
Up tails all!

Kenneth Grahame

A Giggling Gaggle of Geese

Farmyard Poems

MRS HEN AND MRS DUCK

Mrs Hen and Mrs Duck
Went walking out together
They talked about all sorts of things –
The farmyard and the weather.
But all I heard was 'Cluck! Cluck! Cluck!'
And 'Quack! Quack! Quack!' from Mrs Duck.

Anon.

THE DUCK

Behold the duck.
It does not cluck.
A cluck it lacks.
It quacks.
It is specially fond
Of a puddle or pond.
When it dines or sups,
It bottom-ups.

Ogden Nash

WISHES

Said the first little chicken,
With a queer little squirm,
'I wish I could find
A fat little worm.'

Said the second little chicken,
With an odd little shrug,
'I wish I could find
A fat little slug.'

Said the third little chicken,
With a sharp little squeal,
'I wish I could find
Some nice yellow meal.'

'See here,' said the mother,
From the green garden patch,
'If you want any breakfast,
Just come here and SCRATCH.'

Anon.

FLO THE WHITE DUCK

All white and smooth is Flo
A-swimming;
Her lovely dress is plain . . .
No trimming.
A neat delight,
She fans to left and right
The silver rippled pond.
Behind her, safe and fond,
Her yellow ducklings bob and skim,
Yellow, fluffy, trim.

But all a-waddle and a-spraddle goes Flo
A-walking;
A clacking voice she has
For talking.
In slimy ooze
She plants enormous shoes
And squelches, squat and slow.
Behind her, in a row
Her ducklings dip and paddle
And try to spraddle.

Gwen Dunn

THE GIGGLING GAGGLING GAGGLE OF GEESE

The giggling gaggling gaggle of geese,
they keep all the cows and the chickens awake,
they giggle all night giving nobody peace.
The giggling gaggling gaggle of geese.

The giggling gaggling gaggle of geese,
they chased all the ducks and the swans from the lake.
Oh when will the pranks and the noise ever cease
of the giggling gaggling gaggle of geese!

The giggling gaggling gaggle of geese,
it seems there's no end to the mischief they make,
now they have stolen the sheep's woollen fleece.
The giggling gaggling gaggle of geese.

The giggling gaggling gaggle of geese,
they ate all the cake that the farmer's wife baked.
The mischievous geese are now smug and obese.
The giggling gaggling gaggle of geese.

The giggling gaggling gaggle of geese,
eating that cake was a dreadful mistake.
For when holiday comes they will make a fine feast.
The giggling gaggling gaggle of geese.

Jack Prelutsky

DOBBIN

The old horse, Dobbin,
Out at grass
Turns his tail
To the winds that pass;

And stares at the white road
Winding down
Through the dwindling fields
To the distant town.

He hears in the distance,
A snip-snap trot,
He sees his master,
A small dark dot,

Riding away
On the smart new mare
That came last month
From Pulborough Fair.

Dobbin remembers,
As horses may,
How often he trotted
That ringing way.

His coat is ragged
And blown awry.
He droops his head
And he knows not why.

Something has happened.
Something has gone,
The world is changing,
His work is done.

But his old heart aches
With a heavier load
As he stands and wonders
And stares at the road.

Alfred Noyes

THE DONKEY

I saw a donkey
One day old,
His head was too big
For his neck to hold;
His legs were shaky
And long and loose,
They rocked and staggered
And weren't much use.

His face was wistful
And left no doubt
That he felt life needed
Some thinking about.
So he blundered round
In venturesome quest,
And then lay flat
On the ground to rest.

He tried to gambol
And frisk a bit,
But he wasn't quite sure
Of the trick of it.
His queer little coat
Was soft and grey,
And curled at his neck
In a lovely way.

He looked so little
And weak and slim,
I prayed the world
Might be good to him.

Anon.

ODE TO THE PIG: HIS TAIL

My tail is not impressive
But it's elegant and neat.
In length it's not excessive –
I can't curl it round my feet –
But it's awfully expressive,
And its weight is not excessive,
And I *don't* think it's conceit,
Or foolishly possessive
If I state with some agressive-
  ness that it's the final master touch
That makes a pig complete.

Walter R. Brooks

HICKORY, DICKORY, DARE

Hickory, dickory, dare,
The pig flew up in the air.
The man in brown
Soon brought him down,
Hickory, dickory, dare.

Anon.

THE ANSWERS

'When did the world begin and how?'
I asked a lamb,
   a goat,
      a cow.
'What is it all about and why?'
I asked a hog as he went by.
'Where will the whole thing end and when?'
I asked a duck,
   a goose,
      a hen:
And I copied all the answers too,
A quack
   a honk
      an oink
         a moo.

Robert Clairmont

SPRING SONG

On the grass banks
Lambkins at their pranks;
Woolly sisters, woolly brothers,
Jumping off their feet,
While their woolly mothers
Watch by them and bleat.

Christina Rossetti

'QUACK!' SAID THE BILLY-GOAT

'Quack!' said the billy-goat.
'Oink!' said the hen.
'Miaow!' said the little chick
Running in the pen.
'Hobble-gobble!' said the dog.
'Cluck!' said the sow.
'Tu-whit Tu-whoo!' the donkey said.
'Baa!' said the cow.
'Hee-haw!' the turkey cried.
The duck began to moo.
All at once the sheep went,
'Cock-a-doodle-doo!'
The owl coughed and cleared his throat
And he began to bleat.
'Bow-wow!' said the cock
Swimming in the leat.
'Cheep-cheep!' said the cat
As she began to fly.
'Farmer's been and laid an egg –
That's the reason why!'

Charles Causley

COWS ON THE BEACH

Two cows,
fed-up with grass, field, farmer,
barged through barbed wire
and found the beach.
Each mooed to each:
This is a better place to be,
a stretch of sand next to the sea,
this is the place for me.
And they stayed there all day,
strayed this way, that way,
over to rocks,
past discarded socks,
ignoring the few people they met
(it wasn't high season yet).
They dipped hooves in the sea,
got wet up to the knee,
they swallowed pebbles and sand,
found them a bit bland,
washed them down with sea-water,
decided they really ought to
rest for an hour.
Both were sure
they'd never leave here.
Imagine, they'd lived so near
and never knew!
With a swapped moo
they sank into sleep,
woke to the yellow jeep
of the farmer

revving there
feet from the incoming sea.
This is no place for cows to be,
he shouted, and slapped them
with seaweed, all the way home.

Matthew Sweeney

Cows

Half the time they munched the grass, and all
  the time they lay
Down in the water-meadows, the lazy month of May,
A-chewing,
A-mooing,
To pass the hours away.

'Nice weather,' said the brown cow.
'Ah,' said the white.
'Grass is very tasty.'
'Grass is all right.'

Half the time they munched the grass, and all
  the time they lay
Down in the water-meadows, the lazy month of May,
A-chewing,
A-mooing,
To pass the hours away.

'Rain coming,' said the brown cow.
'Ah,' said the white.
'Flies is very tiresome.'
'Flies bite.'

Half the time they munched the grass, and all
  the time they lay
Down in the water-meadows, the lazy month of May,
A-chewing,
A-mooing,
To pass the hours away.

'Time to go,' said the brown cow.
'Ah,' said the white.
'Nice chat.' 'Very pleasant.'
'Night.' 'Night.'

Half the time they munched the grass, and all
  the time they lay
Down in the water-meadows, the lazy month of May,
A-chewing,
A-mooing,
To pass the hours away.

James Reeves

COW IN MEADOW

All day
In a leisurely, kindly sort of way
She crops, and chews the grass,
And watches children as they pass
Through gentle, placid, wondering eyes.
Daylong, under quiet skies
She crops and chews,
Uttering low and melancholy moos
For calves that came, and went again,
And left her lowing in the rain
How many weeks, months, years ago?
Thoughtful and slow
Her jaws work to and fro,
But like a flail
Her urgent, angry tail
Lashes at flies
That settle persistently on flanks and eyes.
All day she munches grass,
And munches grass,
Till the flies go
And evening shadows grow
And young boy's distant cry
'Coo-oo!' joins the rook-noise in the sky.
Then with a lurch she turns her head
Towards the cool, dark milking shed.

Clive Sansom

CHARLIE

In the meadow near our school
A giant carthorse stands,
We feed him crusts and apple cores
From flattened, outstretched hands.

I used to snatch my hand away
From Charlie's lowered head,
I worried that he'd miss my gift
And eat my hand instead.

But now I know his gentleness,
The way he clears my hand,
His muzzle soft as summer grass
Blowing in the wind.

June Crebbin

THE FARMYARD

One black horse standing by the gate,
Two plump cats eating from a plate;
Three big goats kicking up their heels,
Four pink pigs full of grunts and squeals;
Five white cows coming slowly home,
Six small chicks starting off to roam;
Seven fine doves perched upon the shed,
Eight grey geese eager to be fed;
Nine young lambs full of frisky fun,
Ten brown bees buzzing in the sun.

A. A. Attwood

MICE ARE RATHER NICE

Small Creatures and Wildlife

THE FLY

How large unto the tiny fly
Must little things appear!–
A rosebud like a feather bed,
Its prickle like a spear;

A dewdrop like a looking-glass,
A hair like golden wire;
The smallest grain of mustard seed
As fierce as coals of fire;

A loaf of bread, a lofty hill;
A wasp, a cruel leopard;
And specks of salt as bright to see
As lambkins to a shepherd.

Walter de la Mare

THE SNAKE

I hate the snake
I hate the snake
I hate the way it trails and writhes
And slithers on its belly in the dirty dirt and creeps
I hate the snake
I hate its beady eye that never sleeps.

I love the snake
I love the snake

I love the way it pours and glides
And esses through the desert and loops necklaces
   on trees
I love the snake
Its zigs and zags, its ins and outs, its ease.

I hate the snake
I hate the snake
I hate its flickering liquorice tongue
Its hide and sneak, its hissiness, its picnic-wrecking spite
I hate its yawn
Its needle fangs, their glitter and their bite.

I love the snake
I love the snake
I love its coiled elastic names
Just listen to them: hamadryad, bandy-bandy,
   ladder,
Sidewinder, asp
And moccasin and fer de lance and adder

And cascabel
And copperhead
Green mamba, coachwhip, indigo –
So keep your fluffy kittens and your puppy-dogs,
   I'll take
The boomslang and
The anaconda. Oh, I love the snake!

Richard Edwards

EARTH-WORM

Do
you
squirm
when
you
see
an earth-worm?
I never
do squirm
because I think
a big fat worm
is really rather clever
the way it can shrink
and go
so small
without
a sound
into the ground.

And then
what about
all
that
work it does
and no oxygen
or miner's hat?
Marvellous
you have to admit,
even if you don't like fat
pink worms a bit,

how with that
thin
slippery skin
it makes its way
day after day
through the soil,
such honest toil.
And don't forget
the dirt
it eats, I bet
you wouldn't like to come out
at night to squirt
it all over the place
with no eyes in your face:
I doubt
too if you knew
an earth-worm is deaf, but
it can hear YOU go
to and fro
even if you cut
it in half.
So
do not laugh
or squirm
again
when
you
suddenly
see
a worm.

Leonard Clark

BLUE BUTTERFLY

Butterfly,
Blue Butterfly,
all your playground
is the sky,
all your world's
a blaze-of-colour –
blue, rose, emerald,
nothing duller;
touching roses
with your wings,
rising where
a skylark sings
from the garden
to the sky,
there you go,
Blue Butterfly.

Ivy O. Eastwick

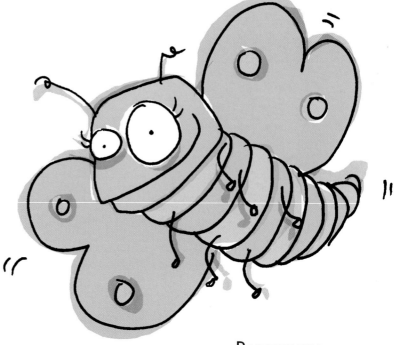

BUTTERFLY

Down the air
He falls sun-lazy
Debonair
Upon a daisy;

Now he drifts
To fall between
Snowy rifts
Of scented bean;

And where petals
Lift in flight,
There he settles
Hid from sight.

S. Thomas Ansell

CATERPILLAR

Creepy crawly caterpillar
Looping up and down,
Furry tufts of hair along
Your back of golden brown.

You will soon be wrapped in silk,
Asleep for many a day;
And then, a handsome butterfly,
You'll stretch and fly away.

Mary Dawson

ONLY IN MY OPINION

Is a caterpillar ticklish?
Well, it's always my belief
That he giggles, as he wiggles
Across a hairy leaf.

Monica Shannon

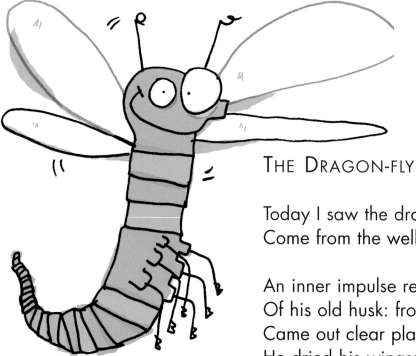

THE DRAGON-FLY

Today I saw the dragon-fly
Come from the wells where he did lie.

An inner impulse rent the veil
Of his old husk: from head to tail
Came out clear plates of sapphire mail.
He dried his wings: like gauze they grew;
Thro' crofts and pastures wet with dew
A living flash of light he flew.

Alfred, Lord Tennyson

HURT NO LIVING THING

Hurt no living thing;
Ladybird, nor butterfly,
Nor moth with dusty wing,
Nor cricket chirping cheerily,
Nor grasshopper so light of leap,
Nor dancing gnat, nor beetle fat,
Nor harmless worms that creep.

Christina Rossetti

BEETLE

A beetle went into a shoe shop
To buy some brand new shoes,
'I'm sorry,' said the assistant,
'But we only sell shoes in twos.'

'But I have six feet,' said the beetle,
'What am I going to do?'
'That's easy,' said the assistant,
Buy two,
… and two,
… and two!'

Andrew Martyr

THE CENTIPEDE

The centipede was happy
Until the toad for fun,
Said, 'Hey, which leg goes after which?'
Which worked his mind to such a pitch
He lay down sadly in a ditch,
Wondering how to run.

Anon.

THE SHARK

A treacherous monster is the Shark
He never makes the least remark.

And when he sees you on the sand,
He doesn't seem to want to land.

He watches you take off your clothes,
And not the least excitement shows.

His eyes do not grow bright or roll,
He has astounding self-control.

He waits till you are quite undrest,
And seems to take no interest.

And when towards the sea you leap,
He looks as if he were asleep.

But when you once get in his range,
His whole demeanour seems to change.

He throws his body right about,
And his true character comes out.

It's no use crying or appealing,
He seems to lose all decent feeling.

After this warning you will wish
To keep clear of this treacherous fish.

His back is black, his stomach white,
He has a very dangerous bite.

Lord Alfred Douglas

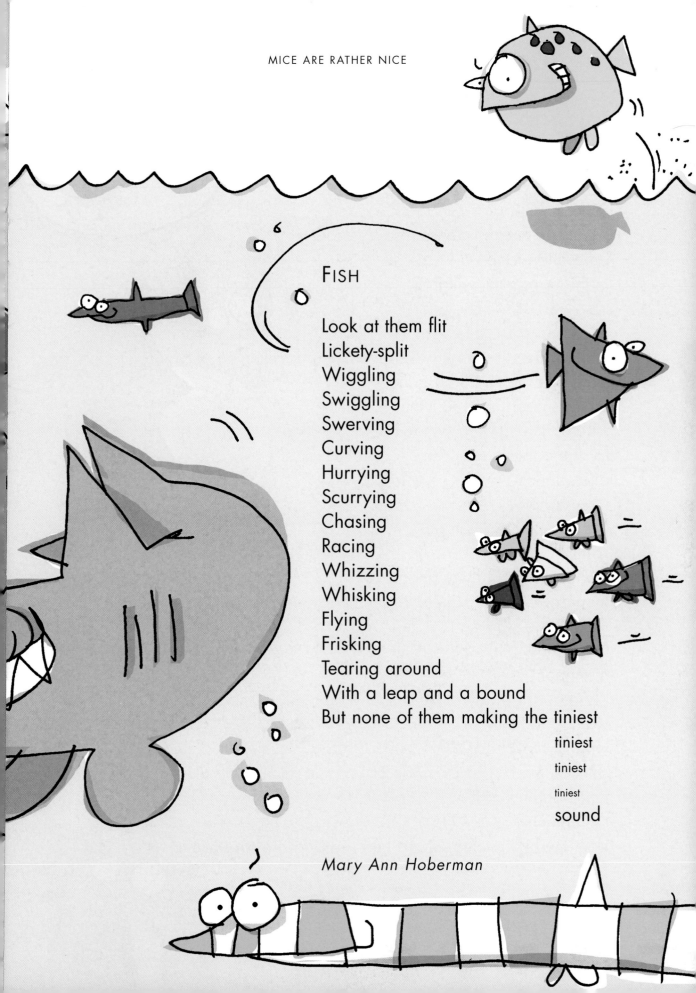

FISH

Look at them flit
Lickety-split
Wiggling
Swiggling
Swerving
Curving
Hurrying
Scurrying
Chasing
Racing
Whizzing
Whisking
Flying
Frisking
Tearing around
With a leap and a bound
But none of them making the tiniest
tiniest
tiniest
sound

Mary Ann Hoberman

LITTLEMOUSE

Light of day going,
Harvest moon glowing,
People beginning to snore,
Tawny owl calling,
Dead of night falling,
Littlemouse opening her door.

Scrabbling and tripping,
Sliding and slipping,
Over the ruts of the plough,
Under the field gate,
Mustn't arrive late,
Littlemouse hurrying now.

Into a clearing,
All the birds cheering,
Woodpecker blowing a horn,
Nightingale fluting,
Blackbird toot-tooting,
Littlemouse dancing till dawn.

Soon comes the morning,
No time for yawning,
Home again Littlemouse creeps,
Over the furrow,
Back to her burrow,
Into bed. Littlemouse sleeps.

Richard Edwards

FOXY COMES TO TOWN

Have you seen the fox in our street
with his rough red hair and his neat sharp feet?

I'd like to hold him, take him in at night
but Dad says he's lousy and Mum says he'd bite.

Sometimes though when I ought to be in bed
I look between my curtains to watch him instead

Creeping on his belly like a soft orange flame.
Then Foxy in the lamplight, I'm glad you're not tame.

Maureen Duffy

85

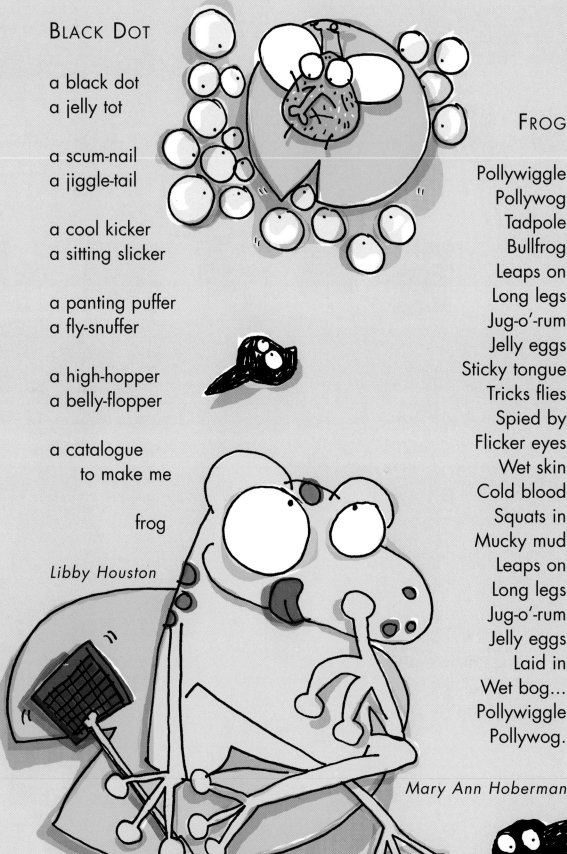

BLACK DOT

a black dot
a jelly tot

a scum-nail
a jiggle-tail

a cool kicker
a sitting slicker

a panting puffer
a fly-snuffer

a high-hopper
a belly-flopper

a catalogue
to make me

frog

Libby Houston

FROG

Pollywiggle
Pollywog
Tadpole
Bullfrog
Leaps on
Long legs
Jug-o'-rum
Jelly eggs
Sticky tongue
Tricks flies
Spied by
Flicker eyes
Wet skin
Cold blood
Squats in
Mucky mud
Leaps on
Long legs
Jug-o'-rum
Jelly eggs
Laid in
Wet bog...
Pollywiggle
Pollywog.

Mary Ann Hoberman

FROGGIE, FROGGIE

Froggie, froggie.
Hoppity-hop!
When you get to the sea
You do not stop.
Plop!

Anon.

THE FROGOLOGIST

I hate it when grown-ups say,
'What do you want to be?'
I hate the way they stand up there
And talk down to me.
I say:
'I want to be a frogologist
And study the lives of frogs,
I want to know their habitat
And crawl about in bogs,
I want to learn to croak and jump
And catch flies with my tongue
And will they please excuse me 'cause
Frogologists start quite young.'

Brian Patten

Croak

DAY OUT

Walking on a low cliff edge,
we watched two seals at sea.
We stared at them—they stared at us,
with expressions of curiosity.
They disappeared and reappeared,
seemed to follow us for a mile or two,
and very soon we began to wonder
just who was watching who.
Perhaps it was *their* day out
and we were exhibits
in their zoo.

Nigel Gray

If Pigs Could Fly

If pigs could fly, I'd fly a pig
To foreign countries small and big –
To Italy and Spain,
To Austria, where cowbells ring,
To Germany, where people sing –
And then come home again.

I'd see the Ganges and the Nile;
I'd visit Madagascar's isle,
And Persia and Peru.
People would say they'd never seen
So odd, so strange an air-machine
As that on which I flew.

Why, everyone would raise a shout
To see his trotters and his snout
Come floating from the sky;
And I would be a famous star
Well known in countries near and far –
If only pigs could fly!

James Reeves

So Big!

The dinosaur, an ancient beast,
I'm told, was very large.
His eyes were big as billiard balls,
His stomach, a garage.
He had a huge and humping back,
A neck as long as Friday.
I'm glad he lived so long ago
And didn't live in my day!

Max Fatchen

Steam Shovel

The dinosaurs are not all dead.
I saw one raise its iron head
To watch me walking down the road
Beyond our house today.
Its jaws were dripping with a load
Of earth and grass that it had cropped.
It must have heard me where I stopped,
Snorted white steam my way,
And stretched its long neck out to see,
And chewed, and grinned quite amiably.

Charles Malam

THE FIERY DRAGON

Oh, the fiery, fiery dragon
Blows fire out through his nose.
But oh, he takes great care, great care,
In case he burns his toes.

Clive Webster

THE LONELY DRAGON

A dragon is sad
Because everyone thinks
A dragon is fierce and brave,
And roars out flames,
And eats everybody,
Whoever comes near his cave.
But a dragon likes people,
A dragon needs friends,
A dragon is lonely and sad,
If anyone knows
Of a friend for a dragon,
A dragon would be very glad.

Theresa Heine

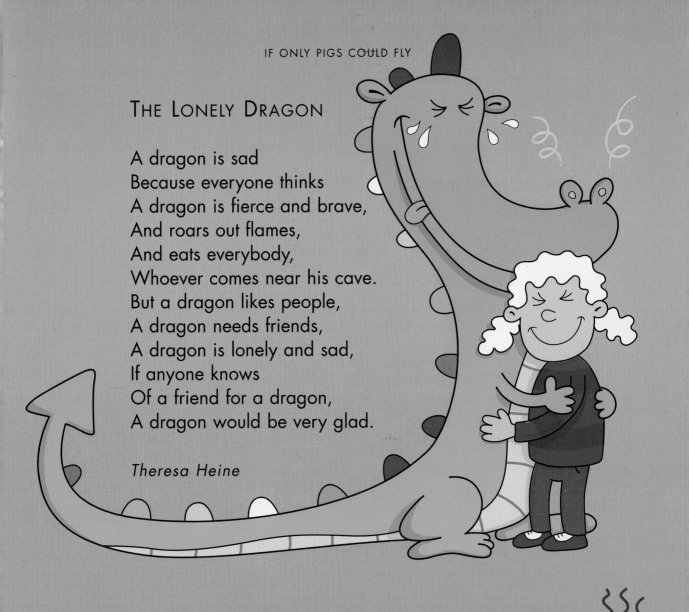

MY FAVOURITE PET

I've got lots of unusual pets
But my dragon's the one I love most,
He wakes me up each day with a roar
And lots of hot buttery toast!

Richard Withers

There was an old lady who swallowed a cow.
I don't know how, she swallowed a cow!
She swallowed the cow to catch the dog.
She swallowed the dog to catch the cat.
She swallowed the cat to catch the bird.
She swallowed the bird to catch the spider,
That wriggled and jiggled and wiggled inside her.
She swallowed the spider to catch the fly,
I don't know why she swallowed a fly,
Perhaps she'll die?

There was an old lady who swallowed a horse.
She's dead of course!

Anon.

THE UNDERWATER CAMEL

The underwater camel
Lives in streams and lakes and pools,
His hobbies are collecting stamps
And jumping over stools.

He likes to wear pyjamas
And play the slide trombone,
And if you ring his number
He'll play it down the 'phone.

Jonathan Allen

99

THREE OF A KIND

I stalk the timberland,
I wreck and splinter through,
I smash log cabins,
I wrestle grizzly bears.
At lunch-time if I'm dry
I drain a lake or two,
I send the wolves and wolverines
Howling to their lairs.
I'm Sasquatch,
Bigfoot,
Call me what you like,
But if you're a backpacker
On a forest hike,
Keep a watch behind you,
I'm there, though rarely seen.
I'm Bigfoot,
Sasquatch,
I'm mean, mean, mean.

I pad across the snow field,
Silent as a thief,
The phantom of the blizzard,
Vanishy, rare.
I haunt the barren glacier
And men in disbelief
Goggle at the footprints
I scatter here and there.
I'm Abominable,
Yeti,

Call me what you choose,
But if you're a mountaineer,
Careful when you snooze,
I'm the restless roaming spirit
Of the Himalayan Range.
I'm Yeti,
Abominable,
I'm strange, strange, strange.

I rear up from the waves,
I thresh, I wallow,
My seven snaky humps
Leave an eerie wake.
I crunch the silly salmon,
Twenty at one swallow,
I tease the silly snoopers –
A fiend? A fish? A fake?
I'm The Monster,
Nessie,
Call me what you please,
But if you're a camper
In the lochside trees,
Before you zip your tent at night
Say your prayers and kneel.
I'm Nessie,
The Monster,
I'm real, real, real.

Richard Edwards

101

THE OWL AND THE PUSSY CAT

The Owl and the Pussy cat went to sea
In a beautiful pea-green boat,
They took some honey and plenty of money,
Wrapped up in a five-pound note.
The Owl looked up to the stars above,
And sang to a small guitar,
'O lovely Pussy! O Pussy, my love,
What a beautiful Pussy you are,
You are
You are!
What a beautiful Pussy you are!'

Pussy said to Owl, 'You elegant fowl!
How charmingly sweet you sing!
O let us be married! Too long have we tarried:
But what shall we do for a ring?'
They sailed away for a year and a day,
To the land where the Bong-tree grows
And there in a wood a Piggy-wig stood
With a ring at the end of his nose,
His nose,
His nose,
With a ring at the end of his nose.

'Dear Pig, are you willing to sell for one shilling
Your ring?' Said the Piggy, 'I will.'
So they took it away, and were married next day
By the Turkey who lives on the hill.
They dined on mince, and slices of quince,
Which they ate with a runcible spoon;
And hand in hand, on the edge of the sand,
They danced by the light of the moon,
The moon,
The moon,
They danced by the light of the moon.

Edward Lear

THE OWL AND THE ASTRONAUT

The owl and the astronaut
Sailed through space
In their intergalactic ship.
They kept hunger at bay
With three pills a day
And drank through a protein drip.
The owl dreamed of mince
And slices of quince
And remarked how life had gone flat;
'It may be all right
To fly faster than light
But I preferred the boat and the cat.'

Gareth Owen

DANIEL AND THE LIONS

The six lions
On the lampshade
In Daniel's midnight room,
Wake up when Daniel's fast asleep
And blink in the gloom,
And shake their manes
And yawn and leap down
Softly to the floor,
Free, as long as darkness lasts,
To prowl round and explore.

Imagine them:
One hunts a spider
Through the carpet pile,
One springs on to the windowsill
To moonbathe for a while,
The others, round
The bedlegs run
Miniature lion races,
But all six jump back up at dawn
To take their usual places
And welcome Daniel
Back from sleep
With the familiar sight
Of six lions on a painted lampshade –
Longing for the night.

Richard Edwards

WANTED – A WITCH'S CAT

Wanted – a witch's cat.
Must have vigor and spite,
Be expert at hissing,
And good in a fight,
And have balance and poise
On a broomstick at night.

Wanted – a witch's cat.
Must have hypnotic eyes
To tantalize victims
And mesmerize spies,
And be an adept
At scanning the skies.

Wanted – a witch's cat,
With a sly, cunning smile,
A knowledge of spells
And a good deal of guile,
With a fairly hot temper
And plenty of bile.

Wanted – a witch's cat,
Who's not afraid to fly,
For a cat with strong nerves
The salary's high.
Wanted – a witch's cat;
Only the best need apply.

Shelagh McGee

 # INDEX OF FIRST LINES